The Underworld in Ancient Mesoamerica: The History and Legacy of Mesoamerican Concepts of Death

By Charles River Editors

Maribel Ponce Ixba's picture of a sculpted head made by the Olmec circa 1200-900 BCE

About Charles River Editors

Charles River Editors is a boutique digital publishing company, specializing in bringing history back to life with educational and engaging books on a wide range of topics. Keep up to date with our new and free offerings with this 5 second sign up on our weekly mailing list, and visit Our Kindle Author Page to see other recently published Kindle titles.

We make these books for you and always want to know our readers' opinions, so we encourage you to leave reviews and look forward to publishing new and exciting titles each week.

Introduction

   The concept of death can be viewed from different perspectives. In general terms, it can be defined as the end of life, but a more spiritual interpretation would describe it as the separation of the soul from the body. Regardless of the definition, death implies change and transformation, even if only on a physical level. The idea of transcendence has served as a source of comfort for humanity that is usually represented in the belief of an afterlife which takes place in another realm.

   Since the beginning of history, understanding and explaining it has been a large concern for people all over the world. Death is both a daily occurrence and an irreversible condition, and countless efforts have been made to avoid or postpone it. The constant struggle to transcend its permanence has led cultures to create the idea of an afterlife; of a place or world where life carries on after its end on earth. In ancient Mesoamerica, this concept of an afterlife greatly permeated the worldview of the many pre-Hispanic cultures that developed all throughout the region.

Among Mesoamericans, life and death were closely related and often deeply integrated, and the two conditions were perceived to exist in an opposition that was at once dynamic and complementary. Described later by the Aztecs as the state of *nepantla*, life and death were viewed by the indigenous people of Mesoamerica as yet another example of the "back and forth" fluctuations common to human life.

Sometimes simplistically described as a borderland or liminal place, *nepantla* is a far more nuanced term and concept. For Mesoamericans there were no "disasters"; life only happened, and the way of that happening was by this back-and-forth, give-and-take model. Since death, killing, and sacrifice were necessary for life and required for nourishment, their necessity was understood and accepted.

The introduction of ancestor worship and rebirth into the equation further clouds modern potential for understanding Mesoamerican conceptions of death. In Mayan communities, deceased ancestors were not buried apart from their families; rather, they were often buried beneath the floor of the family home. In that way, ancestors were included in daily life and were kept apprised of family milestones. Also, ancestors could influence their living descendants or act as intermediaries between the living and the gods. Unhappy or dishonored ancestors could even inflict diseases from the underworld, seen as the source for illness.

Thus, major festivals honored the deceased, and the living sought to commune with them by presenting offerings of food and flowers. This reverence, and attempts to appease departed loved ones, is another example of a ritual which survived the conquest and became an accepted, albeit folk-Catholic, tradition. Originally conducted during late summer (August), post-conquest iterations of the celebrations gradually migrated through the calendar until they coincided with the Catholic celebrations of All Saints' Day and All Souls' Day. Commonly known as the Day of the Dead, this Mesoamerican ancestor-honoring ritual still occurs throughout Latin America, the American Southwest, and anywhere that Latinos with ancestral ties to Mesoamerica live. The physical genuineness of the gifts presented at Day of the Dead shrines, food, drinks, and flowers, mimics the both the content and the idea behind the funeral goods often found in internments of Maya elites.

Like the ancient Egyptians, the Maya believed that the afterlife was a place where the real needs of daily life (like food and money) were necessary, so wealthy Maya elites were buried with an elaborate assortment of funerary goods. Among the goods elites carried with them into death were containers of a cacao-based drink, attendants, dogs, and often large amounts of jade, cloth, and rope. Even poor Maya were buried with a jade bead in their mouths as a bit of currency that they might need in the afterlife.

Furthermore, the underworld in Maya religion is

also associated with foul smells, and often these levels were steaming hot scenes of decay and decomposition where the gods of death lived. The Maya equivalent of the Aztec god of the underworld, Mictlantecuhtli, is referred to as *cizin* or "the flatulent one" in the Madrid Codex (one of the four surviving Maya codices), and Lacondon and Yucatec Maya still refer to the death god as *Cizin* (kee-ZEEN). This god is often depicted as a skeletal figured adorned with strips of paper, a common gift to the dead and when blood soaked, a part of the autosacrificial rituals performed by Maya elites. The depiction of death gods is often animated and suggests a familiarity that borders on affection, as though the certainty of death has rendered the god's existence and powers moot.

Death in the Mesoamerican Worldview

In the pre-Hispanic worldview, death was simply another part of life in which "the immaterial element of the body played a cosmic role in the netherworld that contributed to the functioning of the universe."[1] In contrast to the European system of beliefs, death in ancient Mesoamerica had nothing to do with a person's behavior and the underworld was not a place of punishment. "In the midst of great cultural and regional diversity throughout Mesoamerican history, one clear notion was shared by many if not all peoples: death was more than an occasion for fear, mourning and ritual response; rather, death was perceived as a vital, generative, and creative moment in a cosmic process."[2]

For Mesoamerican people, death was one more step in the course of their life. They considered it the end of a cycle and the beginning of a new one. It was the greatest act of reciprocity towards the gods in which they gave up their bodies and energy as a form of compensation for all they had received in life. After death, a person's soul was said to return

---

[1] Chavez Balderas (2005, p. 7).
[2] Idem (p. 1).

to its source: the Sacred Mountain. There it began a journey through which it was thoroughly cleansed until it could become a new essence that was ready to enter a new body.

After a four-year journey, the deceased's individual existence ran out. The purpose of this journey was to perpetuate the human species. Humans, as all living creatures, possessed a heart which was believed to be indestructible and of a divine nature. In it, the special and essential characteristics of the species were kept, gifted by the god that had created it. When a being died, their heart traveled to the world of the dead and every trace of their individual life was erased. A divine seed was left, ready to be used to create a new being that would live on earth.

The body had three main spiritual entities. The *tonally* was located in the person's head, the *teyolia* corresponded to the heart, and the *ihiyotl* was related to the liver. The *teyolia* was located in the heart where its human essence resided along with its life force, its mental faculties, and its sense of belonging to a kinship group. At the time of death, the *teyolia* traveled to one of the destinations reserved for the dead. Death meant the disintegration and dispersion of the components of the human being. A dead person's destiny was determined by the way in which they died and, in the Nahua tradition, there were four possible places where their soul might go: Mictlan, Tonatiuh Ilhuicac, Tlalocan, or Chichihualcuauhco. For the Maya, this process was slightly different and the dead would travel to Xibalba or the Paradise of the Ceiba. Detailed descriptions of each are discussed below.

The Mesoamerican worldview had a very particular way of understanding the cosmos that relied on the idea of the universe as a cyclical process strongly supported by the concept of duality. This dual and cyclical understanding of the universe considered life to be a synonym of movement, or *ollin* in Nahuatl.[3] The entropy resulting from a loss of energy was believed to be a great danger; therefore, a periodic regeneration of all that existed was necessary. With this in mind, Mesoamericans believed that all forms of life, and

---

[3] Nahuatl is the indigenous language spoken in most of central Mesoamerica. There are currently still some indigenous communities that speak it.

even time, were ruled by cycles of regeneration. This cyclical functioning of the universe required a series of opposing dichotomies that included life and death. For one to exist, the other one was equally necessary.

In pre-Hispanic cosmology, everything was tied to supernatural implications, including the human body. Death belonged to this dynamic and was viewed, not as something fatal as in most cultures, but as a process of renewal. All across Mesoamerica, "death and all beings connected to it [were] associated with the creation of individuals, of peoples, and of humanity as a whole. Its name was given to one of the days of the Maya calendar, *Cimi*, and had its Mexica counterpart in *Miquiztli*."[4] In the Maya worldview, death was consubstantial to life. These two opposing forces represented order and chaos, light and darkness, sky and underworld, masculine and feminine, rationality and irrationality. Together, they created harmony which was fundamental in the composition of the cosmos. For the ancient Maya, the balance between life and death was kept by sacred forces under the control of

____

[4] Chavez Balderas (2005, p. 1).

gods that lived in the sky and in the underworld, two realms of opposing forces. The lords of death were mainly represented as anthropomorphic beings.

Life and death were created by sacred forces that dwelt in the sky and underworld, respectively. In the sky, the sun travels bringing light and heat. The daily and yearly cycles were formed to generate time and, along with it, the rain season that fertilized the earth to produce life. In contrast, the underworld is the realm of darkness and death. Disease and evil surge from it and it houses the souls of the dead. Despite the many apparently negative associations to the underworld, not all is bad; the underworld holds great mineral treasures, sacred springs, and seeds that will bring new life. The Earth, located between the two realms, is the place where life and death battle, where the opposing forces clash and harmonize. Earth is the realm of man, the center of the universe where opposites become one.

Death was connected to many things in the pre-Hispanic worldview, but one of the most important was maize. As the base of the Mesoamerican sustenance, maize was a fundamental component of all aspects of life, including death. "Death received ritual blood offerings because it was believed that—like the sun in the sky—death, wherever it resided or manifested itself, ensured the continuity of life."[5] Death received seeds, since they are placed beneath the earth in a similar way to how dead bodies are buried. The process of renewal and rebirth took place in the underworld and allowed life to emerge anew on Earth. Several myths from different Mesoamerican cultures share the notion of life being generated from the land of the dead, such as the Nahua story in which Quetzalcoatl stole bones from the underworld to create the human race, and the section of the *Popol Vuh* that narrates how the "Hero Twins" were conceived in Xibalba.

The Mesoamerican Underworld

The underworld was generally considered "a fearsome and dreaded place named *Mictlan* by the Aztec, and *Xibalba* or "place of fright" by the K'iche' Maya, and was the place through which all souls, save those killed violently (for example victims of warfare), were required to journey after

____

[5] Idem.

death."[6] To fully understand the concept of the Mesoamerican underworld, it is necessary to comprehend it in terms of the entire pre-Hispanic cosmic geography and not as an isolated realm. The celestial and earthly realms worked together with the underworld to create the functioning universe. All three planes were connected and depended on the others.

At the time of the Spanish conquest, the majority of the native population conceived of the underworld as consisting of nine levels.[7] This is congruent with the evidence recovered archaeologically. The most detailed description of the Nahua underworld can be found in "the Aztec Codex Vaticanus A in which the first layer is part of the inhabitable earth. Layers continue downward, descending into the passage of waters, followed by the entrance to mountains, hill of obsidian knives, place of frozen winds, place where the flags tremble, place where people are flayed, place where the hearts of people are devoured, and finally to the ninth layer, referred to as *Mictlan Opochcalocan*,

---

[6] Moyes (2013).

[7] Idem.

where the dead lie in eternal darkness. (…) These layers are reminiscent of the torture "houses" that the Hero Twins must endure in the Maya *Popol Vuh* story, an ethnohistoric account of the Maya creation myth."[8]

As narrated in the Popol Vuh, "the underworld was inhabited by the Lords of the Underworld, who were denizens of death, disease, and violence that prayed on human frailty. In the story, pairs of Hero Twins traveled deep into the underworld to encounter the evil lords, navigating the rivers and trails that lead to the lowest levels."[9]

In ancient Mesoamerica, smells were linked to primordial cosmic beliefs. Many pre-Hispanic societies conceived the underworld to be a foul-smelling place. The Maya, in particular, imagined the entrance to the land of the dead like the mouth of a cave that reeked of decomposing bodies, so much so in fact that the god that dwelt there was known for his farts and for consuming rotten waste.

In central Mexico, Mictlan was conceived as an

---

[8] Idem.
[9] Idem.

inversion of the land of the living, a belief that persists among several indigenous communities in the present. In a passage written by Fray Bernardino de Sahagun[10] it is said that the inhabitants of Mictlan ate everything that was not eaten on earth, in particular, tamales filled with an insect called *pinacate* which is known to cause extreme flatulence. Some codices even show the gods of Mictlan eating excrement.

In general terms, Mesoamerican cultures perceived the universe as a superposition of horizontal planes that can be grouped into three realms, each of which contained a specific number of planes. The celestial realm contained thirteen planes, the earth's surface corresponded to one plane, and the underworld had nine planes. Each one of these planes was held up by five pillars that were represented in the forms of gods or cosmic trees. Four pillars were places at the cardinal points and one in the center. On the horizontal plane, the earth's surface formed a square divided into four quadrants by diagonal lines. This division represented the sun's trajectory who indicated that the north corresponded to his right

____

[10] See Dupey Garcia (2015).

and the south to his left since he traveled west. This general belief was shared by most groups; however, the meaning attributed to the north and south varied from one culture to another. For the Aztecs, for example, the north was typically associated to Mictlan. For other cultures, like the Maya, the underworld was located to the south. Regardless of the cardinal direction, the relevant factor here is that many burials were oriented towards where the culture in question believed the underworld to be.[11]

The orientation of burials can tell us a lot about the pre-Hispanic worldview. The cardinal directions were related to certain gods and to parts of the underworld. The orientation of a body depended on the way the person had died and, therefore, to the level of the underworld they would go to. According to the myths, north corresponds to the deepest level of the underworld, in the nadir of the vital cycle. The south, in contrast, is consecrated by the birth of Huitzilopochtli represented by the zenith of the cycle.

In mythical terms, the opposition between north

---

[11] See Pereira (2010).

and south, nadir and zenith, expresses the duality between feminine and masculine represented by the gods Coyolxauhqui and Huitzilopochtli.

The east represents the daytime dimension of life or existence and it corresponds to the highest elevation possible in any cycle (sun, human life, and plant life, etc.). The west marks the end of existence and the reintegration into the warmth of the earth, the dimension where life gestates again. Just as the sun rises in the east from the entrails of the earth, transforming the night into day, evolving and culminating in the zenith, so does man as he is born in the east, leaving behind his nocturnal state to enter the daylight dimension of his life which concludes in the west with the return of the essential night: death. The beliefs about death and the different places where the dead would roam derive from this concept.

The belief in a world composed of three realms corresponded, in some Mesoamerican cultures, to concepts of time, namely the temporal dimension marked by the sun's journey. During this path, time moved very slowly and only certain individuals like priests or ritual specialists were able to access this dimension during certain ceremonies or dreams. In the case of the underworld, communicating with ancestors was a very important practice that was carried out for several purposes, for example, to seek out guidance or favor, especially in the event of a war or natural disaster.

The movement in time and space carried out by the sun while, at the same time, defining the cardinal directions, also defines the four places where the dead go to. The first of these and the most common is known as *Mictlan* or the "Place of the Dead," realm of Mictlantecuhtli, Lord of the Dead. All those who died of natural causes were sent here and, in *Mictlan* souls, lived pretty much the same way they did on earth. The bodies of those destined for this realm were buried with everything they would need in the afterlife; burials typically contained pottery and tools. *Mictlan* was believed to be oriented to the north, though it didn't really correspond to a specific place. Instead, it was a dark area located below the earth that ran in a north-south direction and was limited by the east and west.

The second place was the paradise of the sun, also known as the *Tonatiuh Ilhuicac* or "House of the Sun." This was the realm of Huitzilopochtli, the god of war, and those who had a glorious death, either in battle or by sacrifice, were sent there. The *Tonatiuh Ilhuicac* was located in the sky and was divided in two parts, the east and the west. In addition to warriors, merchants who died carrying out their duties were also sent there since they typically also served as war spies. Women who died in childbirth also went to the *Tonatiuh Ilhuicac* because giving birth was considered a battle. These women were known as *mocihuaquetzques*. All the souls of the House of the Sun became companions of the sun and helped to transport him across the skies; from dawn to noon the sun was carried by warriors and from noon to dusk by the *mocihuaquetzques*.

The third place was the *Tlalocan* or the paradise of Tlaloc, the rain god. All of those who died in relation to water, such as people who drowned, those who were struck by lightning, or those who died of illnesses that they associated to water such as leprosy, scabies, gout, hydropsy, and yaws went to the *Tlalocan*. It was a place of eternal rebirth and abundance located in the east.

The fourth place was the *Chichihualcuauhco* or nursing tree, a realm for dead infants that still did not consume maize and had, therefore, not been contaminated by "dead nature." Here, the children waited their turn to be reborn.

In the Mesoamerican worldview, life gestated in the silent and dark dimension of death, in places such as Mictlan, Cumiehchucuaro, Metnal, and Xibalba. Within the Nahua myth of the creation of man, there is a clear association of death to the maternal womb. The myth narrates that the god, Quetzalcoatl, descended into the depths in search of jade-bones. During this process, Quetzalcoatl's male essence entered the female receptacle conceived as a conch shell. The shell was then "deflowered" by worms and the sound made by the shell entered the ears of Mictlantecuhtli, Lord of Mictlan.

Similar associations can be seen in the *Popol Vuh* in passages like the decapitation of Hun Hunahpu and the fruition of the dry tree afterwards, and the fertilization of Xquic by the spermatic saliva contained in the gourd and the subsequent birth of the twins Hunahpu and Xbalanque.[12]

Ethnohistorical accounts also say that Nahua midwives believed that unborn babies were still in Mictlan; therefore, a pregnant woman's belly was comparable to the underworld, just as Mictlan was considered to be a space of regeneration.

In the Nahua culture, there were many deities associated to death; one of the most curious was Tlaltecuhtli, Lord/Lady of the Earth. This deity was in charge of devouring the dead individual, regardless of how they had died, meaning that the deceased had to be eaten by the earth both in a literal and symbolic way. In the pre-Hispanic worldview, the flesh and blood of the dead were necessary to feed the Sun and the Earth. Evidence of this belief can be found on codices and ethnohistorical accounts.

Once the individual was devoured, they passed into the womb of Tlaltecuhtli where a rite of passage took place. Here, the essence of the deceased would be birthed so that it could begin its journey to its final destination. This is why the goddess is

---

[12] See Johansson (2003).

depicted with her legs spread open as if giving birth and, in this way, the duality of life and death was represented through the concepts of devouring and birthing.

Architecture

There are many sites, particularly throughout the Maya area, where the architecture clearly reflects a connection to the underworld. One place where this can be seen is in Palenque; the Pyramid of the Inscriptions has nine levels (making reference to the nine levels of the underworld). The last level is the deepest and contains the tomb of Pakal, making a clear analogy to Xibalba being located in the ninth level. A similar thing can be found in Tikal, where Temple I also contains nine levels and the tomb of a ruler.

"Monster-temples" are other architectural elements found mainly in the Maya area that make a clear reference to the underworld. These structures emulate the jaws of the Earth monster which represents the entrance to Xibalba. Examples of this can be found at sites like Tonina, Ek Balam, and Becan.

In central Mesoamerica, there is also evidence of architecture with a direct link to the underworld. The Aztec capital of Tenochtitlan had a central dual pyramid called Templo Mayor, dedicated to the gods Huitzilopochtli and Tlaloc. For the Aztecs, this building represented the center of the universe and it was the place from which you could ascend the levels of the celestial realm or descend into the underworld. The two pyramids were representations of the two sacred mountains the soul had to cross in order to begin the four year journey. Pre-Hispanic codices and ethnohistorical sources mention the two mountains that the dead had to cross on their way to Mictlan.

Many Mesoamerican cultures show evidence of a connection between the ballgame and the underworld. The game was a symbolic battle between the lords of death and the representatives of the sun or maize. In the end, the lords of death were always victorious and their rivals were sacrificed only to resurrect later on after going through the trials of the underworld.

While the ballgame was a source of sport and

entertainment in ancient Mesoamerica, it also had important symbolic associations. Some scholars have suggested that the movement of the ball across the court is analogous to the movement of the sun across the sky. In this view, the ballgame represents a battle between day and night, when the sun must pass through the underworld before rising again at dawn. Closely connected to this idea is the theme of agricultural fertility; this is ensured through the movement of celestial bodies, which create seasons and rainfall. Ballcourts were also thought of as connections to the underworld. In the Maya area, surviving texts indicate the ballgame was the setting for mythological battles between the forces of life and death. Painted ceramic vases and carved stone sculptures show kings dressed as gods reenacting these mythological games.[13]

In general terms, Mesoamerican cultures believed that access to the afterlife was possible through several geographical features such as caves, lagoons, and *cenotes*,[14] and nebulous places, among

____

[13] Earley (2017).

others. These portals allowed the deceased to travel to the different realms where the dead resided.

Caves had many meanings for ancient Mesoamericans: a refuge, a place of dwelling, the mouth of the Earth, a womb, an entrance to the underworld, the house of the gods of water and death, the place of origin, and a place of worship. Caves are often mentioned in myths and represented in codices and are deeply linked to the pre-Hispanic worldview. For Nahua groups that lived in central Mesoamerica, the sun and moon were believed to have emerged from a cave, and the Aztecs were said to have been one of the seven tribes that came out of the mythical cave called Chicomoztoc. Another myth even narrates that Quetzalcoatl went underground to steal corn from the ants and bring food up to earth. In this section, however, we will focus on the connection between caves and the underworld.

In Mesoamerica, caves were rarely used as homes or dwellings, instead their function was sacred and they were places where celebrations and rituals were

---

[14] Cenotes are deep natural occurring pits filled with water. They can be found mainly in Yucatan and were used by the ancient Maya for different purposes, including rituals, sacrifices, and fresh water.

carried out, mainly in relation to the dead. "Throughout Mesoamerica, caves take on a special meaning that may vary between cultures, but share common themes surrounding life, fertility, and abundance juxtaposed with those of danger, evil, and death. In Mesoamerican thought, both in the past and present, caves are ambiguous spaces associated with indwelling good and evil deities that can be coaxed, flattered, or angered by humans. It is for this reason that rituals in caves were used as a place to petition and honor these deities so vital to human well-being."[15]

Caves were considered to be entrances to the underworld. "Both the Maya and the Aztecs viewed their world as consisting of three levels: the sky, the middle world or earth, and the underworld. Classic period glyphic associations for ancient Maya caves contain elements such as a skull, bone, mandible, or detached eye within a half darkened field, suggesting affiliations with death and the underworld."[16] There is evidence to suggest that journeys into caves were likely a reenactment of the

____

[15] Moyes (2013).
[16] Idem.

soul's passage through the underworld. In the Maya area, these journeys may have represented that of the Hero Twins and were possibly considered rites of passage.

As an entrance to the land of the dead, caves were also funerary chambers. The relationship between the underworld and the female womb also made caves the access into the earth's belly and the place where fertility could be propitiated. "Research on ancient Mesoamerican sacred landscapes has highlighted the importance of the sacred earth in pre-Hispanic religions. (…) As literal geographic entrances into the earth, caves are one of the most salient features of the sacred landscape because they reify the cosmology of this three-tiered universe representing a conduit between the middle world of humans and the underworld."[17]

The presence of caves, as well as other natural geographical features such as springs and volcanoes, was an important element Mesoamerican societies took into consideration when choosing locations for new settlements because these features possessed

____

[17] Moyes (2012, p. 8).

direct connections to the other realms, including the underworld. Many important sites were built near a cave or over tunnels due to the important link these features had to the underworld.[18] Teotihuacan, for example, was seemingly constructed over a large system of tunnels that run underneath the site's main pyramids. Xochicalco is another site that was built in direct relation to tunnels. In some Mesoamerican sites, these tunnels contain springs or underground rivers, which were also features associated to the underworld. The great pyramid of Cholula was erected directly over a sacred spring, indicating its immediate connection to the Land of the Dead.

The oldest representation of a cave was found on a monument at Chalcatzingo that is carved into a large boulder on the side of a mountain. "In the carving, a personage, possibly a religious leader, ruler, or ancestor wearing an elaborate headdress is shown sitting inside of a cave on a throne or bench that has a symbol for a cloud inscribed on it. In his arms rests an object resembling a ceremonial bar that is also marked with a cloud symbol. Mist or smoke emanates from the cave, as plants and vegetation

____

[18] See Manzanilla (2021).

spring up around the entrance and clouds rain on the scene."[19] The association between caves and rain can be seen all across Mesoamerica, and even rain gods like Cocijo, Tlaloc, and Chaac were believed to dwell there. Caves were, additionally, important spaces for the enactment of rituals that endowed leaders with political power. The access to communicate with underworld deities was, surely, a feat only the most powerful could achieve.

Archaeological evidence points to the ritual use of caves since the Preclassic period, which provides clear indication of the importance they had since the first complex societies emerged in Mesoamerica. The use of caves throughout all of the chronological periods is well documented. Some of the earliest evidence found in caves suggests that they were used as places for ceremonial burials. Bones associated to important ancestors were often deposited in these spaces and offerings would be frequently left to honor the sacred lineages. The connection between caves and ancestors can be found in many pre-Hispanic cultures, such as the Mixtec, Zapotec, Nahua, Otomi, and Maya, among

---

[19] Moyes (2013).

others.

Different kinds of ritual burials were made in caves. Not only children sacrificed in honor of the rain god met their end in the small chambers of caves, but also the skins of flayed bodies from *tlacaxipehualiztli,*[20] the Aztec ritual in which priests removed the hearts and skin of sacrificial victims, were kept in caves. This suggests that there was a relation between death and fertility since seed begin their life underground in the darkness. The bodies of two women sacrificed to Xochiquetzal, the goddess of plants and love, were also kept underground in an *ayauhcalli* or "house of fog."

Natural caves were often modified to be used as places of ritual and worship. Evidence of architecture and human intervention has been found in caves all across the Mesoamerican territory. One of the most impressive examples is the cave at Las Cuevas, Belize, where the entrance was modified with terraces, walls, stairs, and platforms. The size and location of the cave, combined with the archaeological evidence found, has led researchers

---

[20] See Heyden (1998).

to believe that it was used as a ritual site and pilgrimage center that emulated the descent into the different levels of the underworld.

Cave constructions recreated cosmic space, reified cosmological principles, and enhanced the embodied experience for the ancient users. Architectural constructions in the tunnel system of Las Cuevas structured a narrative for participants as they moved through the space. These elaborations not only separated the earth from the underworld, but also defined levels of descent as participants moved deeper into the cave. By taking human experience and embodiment into account, architecture is envisioned not as static piles of rock that partition space, but as dynamic constructions that created, directed, and structured the ancient journey through the underworld.[21]

For the ancient Maya, caves symbolized the womb or the primordial cavity that produced life. Surrounded by permanent darkness, the cave remained untouched by the ordering principles of

---

[21] Moyes (2012, p. 20).

the earth's surface and the celestial realm. It was a space of death and resurrection. Ruled by the gods of night, the cave became the entrance to the world under the surface: the underworld, the jaws of the mountain. The stalactites and stalagmites were viewed as the sharp teeth of the monstrous entity. Not only dark beings lived in caves, deities of fertility like Chaac, the rain god, and the goddess of the moon, birth, and medicine also dwelt in them. The Maya believed that when the moon disappears over the horizon, she went to sleep in a cave only to resurface again the following night.

  During pre-Hispanic times, particularly during the Classic Period, many caves in the Maya region became destinations for pilgrimages and were used as places where intense ritual activities took place. Common ceremonies included making offerings of food and incense to the gods, human sacrifice, fertility rites, and funerary practices. Some caves conserve images and hieroglyphs that reveal the identities of those who worshiped in them. Many caves in Yucatan preserve paintings of gods related to death, including one in which a deity appears to be holding a torch as if he were welcoming the newly dead into the underworld.[22]

Mictlan

Mictlan was the place where the souls of all those who had died of natural or common causes went. On the road to Mictlan, the soul had to cross the nine levels of the underworld. They were accompanied by a dog that had to have a reddish color, never white or black, so that it could help them cross the Apanohuaya river. This was only the first trial. Those that followed also contained difficult tests that would cleanse the deceased.

According to the Spanish chronicler Sahagun, those bodies that were destined for Mictlan were burned and their ashes were placed in a jar or pot and were buried beneath one of the rooms of their household. After four years the dead person's essence left the body and began its journey to the land of the dead. As was mentioned above, Mesoamericans believed that the human body possessed a kind of soul related to the heart which was called *teyolia*. This entity was the one that journeyed to the underworld.

____

[22] See Bernal Romero (2008).

There are two numbers associated with the underworld - four and nine. The four-year journey corresponds to the four years the body was buried in a pot. As mentioned above, the body was cremated first, action which symbolically fed the Earth and the Sun. After the four years, the *teyolia* had to cross nine steps to reach Mictlan. Some researchers[23] believe that there is a connection between these nine levels and the nine months of human gestation. In addition, Mictlan has also been compared to a womb.

The literal translation for the term Mictlan is "place of the dead," from the Nahuatl words *micca*, which means "dead," and *tlan*, which means "place of."[24] In the sources, it is depicted as a dark, dangerous, and unknown place. The "House of Darkness" or "House of Night," as it was also called, was associated to the number nine since the deceased had to cross nine levels to reach their final destination. The underworld was typically described as cold, damp, fetid, wet, and putrid. Gods and

---

[23] See Matos Moctezuma (2013).
[24] Luna Lopez (2017).

animals dwelt there under the rule of Mictlantecuhtli.

Though the information on the nine levels of the underworld is quite scarce, the sources do agree that each level presented a sort of trial that the deceased had to go through in order to continue their journey. The entire process can be considered a road back to the point of origin, particularly if the idea of a cyclical universe is considered. Mictlan was not a place of punishment and despair as one might be inclined to believe, it was a place of regeneration and rebirth. That is why the underworld is often associated to the female womb and pregnancy. A clear analogy can be traced between the nine levels of the underworld and the nine months of pregnancy, the end result being the same: new life.

The negative ideas that were associated to the Mesoamerican concept of the underworld were clear misinterpretations made by the Spanish. Many pre-Hispanic deities and beliefs were considered to be representation of hell due to the imagery they presented. For the Catholic conquistadors, skulls, bones, blood, human sacrifice, and the like were things they immediately associated with the devil. In this sense, Mictlan was assumed to be hell.

There are two main ethnohistorical sources that describe the nine levels of Mictlan, the *Codice Florentino*, written by Fray Bernardino de Sahagun, and the *Codex Vaticanus* or *Codice Rios,* written under the supervision of Fray Pedro de los Rios.

The Codex Vaticanus contains the most detailed description of the nine layers of Mictlan, "in which the first layer is part of the inhabitable earth. One then descends into the passage of waters, followed by the entrance to mountains, hill of obsidian knives, place of frozen winds, place where the flags tremble, place where people are flayed, place where the hearts of people are devoured, and finally to the ninth layer, referred to as Mictlan Opochcalocan, where the dead lie in eternal darkness."[25]

Nine areas had to be crossed in order to reach this region, which was located under the earth. The deceased was left all necessary items for his or her journey. The route is described in the Codice Vaticano Latino 3738 (Vatican Latin

____

[25] Moyes (2012, pp. 10-11).

Codex 3738). The first stop was the Chiconahuapan River, where a brownish dog awaited his master to help him across. After the crossing, the deceased ascend through a region where mountains crashed into each other. Later, he or she would face the Obsidian Mountain, and then a place where the wind was so cold that it cut like a knife. The blankets given to the dead during the funeral would help in this stage. The deceased next had to cross a place where flags wave in order to reach the place where people are pierced by arrows. More dangers awaited upon his or her arrival in the place where wild animals eat human hearts. After four years, the journey was completed with the arrival at Mictlan, a dark, windowless place ruled by Mictlantecuhtli and his wife Mictecacíhuatl. The god of the underworld was a semi-skeletal being, with curly hair and a nose made of a flint knife.[26]

Descriptions of Mictlan are also scarce; however, Sahagun includes this brief passage that provides some information on the matter. It was said that in

---

[26] Chavez Balderas (2005, p. 5).

the Land of the Dead:

the obsidian knives are carried off by the wind

the sand is carried off by the wind

the trees are carried off by the wind

[there are] Cereus garambullo cacti

the flintstone knives are carried off by the wind

[there are] Mexican agaves

[there are] brambles

it is very cold

[there are] ferrocactli…[27]

Another passage of the *Codice Florentino*, in the Nahuatl section, makes reference to Mictlan and Mictlantecuhtli:

[he destroyed them, he hid them], our lord

[the old men, the old women ("the ancestors")]

[…] he sent them

[into the water, to the cave] to Mictlan

---

[27] Sahagun cited in Mikulska (2015, p. 140).

they are resting now/getting cold

[there close to his side]

of [our mother, our father]

Mictlantecuhtli[28]

<u>Mictlantecuhtli</u>

The most well-known character associated with the underworld is Mictlantecuhtli, the Aztec god of death who was also worshipped throughout most of central Mesoamerica. Together with his wife Mictecacihuatl, he ruled over Mictlan. Mictlantecuhtli is typically depicted as a skeleton with gruesome claws and bulging eyes, or as a body covered in bones with red spots symbolizing blood. Sometimes he is shown wearing a skull mask, a sacrificial knife instead of a nose, bone earplugs, an owl costume or a necklace made of eyeballs. Sacrifices were made in his honor and the blood of the sacrificial victim would be poured over life-size statues of the god. Images of Mictlantecuhtli have been found on many codices, as well as statues and sculptures.

---

[28] Sahagun cited in Mikulska (2015, p. 116), translation mine.

The Borgia Codex contains an image that represents the inside of the earth or the Land of the Dead.[29] The deceased walk through the mouth of the earth monster to then find themselves in front of the Lord of the Dead who is depicted in the company of owls – described as messengers of the underworld in several sources – and body parts that were meant to be food for the lords that dwelt in these parts.

When Europeans saw the images of Mictlantecuhtli, they automatically associated them with their own Christian conceptions of death; however, it is important to remember that the role of Mictlantecuhtli was entirely different to that of the Grim Reaper. As Haly adequately states, "I am trying to overcome our resistance to seeing the deity who created life as the 'Lord of the Land of the Dead.' This distinction is easier for us if we disassociate the skeletal figure of Omiteuctli/Mictlanteuctli from that of the Grim Reaper. The 'Lord of the Land of the Dead' is not 'Death' itself. Or if he is, he is also 'Life.' In Mesoamerica, death precedes life."[30]

---

[29] See Mikulska (2015).
[30] Haly (1992, p. 286) cited in Mikulska (2015, p. 136).

Xibalba

Xibalba is the most commonly used name for the Maya underworld; however, for the Yucatec Maya it was called Metnal. The term Xibalba means "place of fright," making reference to the darkness that ruled over it. Contrary to what some might believe, Xibalba (like Mictlan discussed above) was not the equivalent of the Christian concept of Hell; all the dead, except for those who died a violent death, went to Xibalba.

There are a few similarities between Xibalba and Mictlan, for example, they both housed the souls of all those who died of natural causes and they both consisted of nine levels. Also, as with Mictlan, water was an element that was strongly associated to Xibalba. The watery quality of the Maya underworld is evidenced by the presence of aquatic elements like reptiles, fish, turtles, frogs, and water lilies.

As was the case with Mictlan, the Maya underworld also consisted of nine levels but organized in a different way: four steps descended down the western horizon to the nadir of the fifth level, and four additional steps ascended to the eastern horizon. The ninth level corresponded to the "Land of the Dead". "There is a deity associated with each level, and the underworld gods are considered to be malevolent, bringing evil and death to humans. These deities roam the earth at night and reenter the underworld through caves at daybreak where they are thought to make their homes."[31] To reach the ninth level of the underworld, the deceased had to go through a series of difficult trials like crossing dangerous mountains and rivers and surviving violent attacks by flying obsidian blades. The dead were typically buried with objects that would help them overcome these trials; weapons, tools, amulets, food, and even dogs can be commonly found in Maya burials.

Xibalba was ruled by a group of gods known as the Lords of the Underworld. Some accounts identify nine gods, while others fourteen. Some of these lords were believed to have the ability to come up to earth and spread disease and misery among the living. In addition, each astronomical god had a manifestation in the underworld, for example, the

____

[31] Moyes (2012, p. 11).

Sun God became the Jaguar God at night as he traveled through the underworld. "According to the Popol Vuh, [Xibalba] was inhabited by the Lords of the Underworld, denizens of death, disease, and violence that preyed on human frailty. In the myth, the Hero Twins traveled deep into the underworld to encounter the evil lords, navigating the rivers and trails that lead to the lowest levels."[32]

Xibalba was also inhabited by human-like beings, which corresponded to the souls of those who died on the earthly realm, and by the Maize God. In the *Popol Vuh*, "Hun Hunahpu, the father of the Hero Twins was transformed into the Maize God, and was left in the underworld to dwell and receive offerings, cyclically emerging into the middle world as the maize plant each growing season."[33]

A lot of the information available on Xibalba comes from the *Popol Vuh*. The following excerpt summarizes the most important myth the Maya have in relation to the underworld.

One of the most celebrated stories involves the

---

[32] Idem (p. 10).
[33] Moyes (2012, p. 10).

Maize God (Hun Hunahpu or 1 Ajaw) and his brother 7 Hunahpu. Playing a noisy game of ball one day, the pair angered the lords of the underworld who summoned them to descend into Xibalba. After suffering many trials and horrors, the siblings played another game of ball. This time, on losing the game, they were sacrificed and buried under the ballcourt, whilst the Maize God's head was placed in a calabash or cacao tree. Later, a daughter of one of the lords of the underworld, Blood Maiden, saw the head and, after a little conversation and with the head spitting in her hand, she miraculously became pregnant with twins. These siblings were Hunahpu (or Hun Ajaw) and Xbalanque (or Yax Bahlam), the famous Hero Twins of Maya mythology, who would gain fame as great hunters, practical jokers and superb ball players.

  History repeated itself and the Hero Twins, like their father and uncle, were also summoned into Xibalba and, after being held captive in terrible chambers with Death Bats, jaguars, terrible cold, and fires, were also made to play a game of ball. This they won, but it did them no good as they were executed anyway, or rather, the lords of the underworld hoped to kill them, but the twins acted first and leapt into a tremendous fire. However, the gods of the outer world were not best pleased at this result, and so they brought the twins back to life. Now disguised as dancers, the pair wreaked havoc in Xibalba, slew the lords of the underworld, and even managed to resurrect their father the Maize God. The three, along with a bevy of naked maidens and now laden with treasure, then used a canoe to finally escape from Xibalba and return to the land of the living.[34]

Evidence of the myths concerning Xibalba can also be found on pottery, cave paintings, and engraved stones. The Lords of the Underworld are depicted in gruesome detail with their eyes hanging out of their sockets and flesh falling off their bones.

The Maya believed that Xibalba was located to the far west and it could be accessed through caves or bodies of still water on *Tlalticpac*, the earth's

---

[34] Cartwright (2014).

surface. *Tlalticpac* was considered the first of the nine levels of the underworld. Xibalba could also be entered by following the Milky Way's path.

It was believed that the entrance to Xibalbá was in Guatemala and that, in order to reach it, one had to descend a steep staircase before crossing a river with a strong current that flowed between thorny calabash trees. Along the way, the deceased encountered another river, the river of pus, and then moved towards a river of blood and another one of water. The latter was located between two steep cliffs. Soon afterwards, the traveler would be at the junction of four roads, and only the black one would lead to Xibalbá, where the council chamber of the lords of the underworld was located. It was also the site of a garden with birds and flowers, and of a ballcourt. There was also a spring that was the source of a river and six houses that were torture chambers. Hun Camé and Vucub Camé were the supreme gods of this region, although there were other lords who caused illness and death.[35]

---

[35] Chavez Balderas (2005, p. 6).

Spanish chroniclers like Diego de Landa and Bartolome de Las Casas[36] as well as the *Popol Vuh,* a 16th century text written by the Quiche Maya, documented the Maya beliefs concerning the underworld. They believed that the entrance to the underworld was through a cave located at Carcha, close to the site of Coba in Guatemala. The descent to Xibalba, the Land of the Dead, was full of difficult trials that the deceased had to successfully traverse. The journey began with stairs that were said to be very steep; the following trials included a river with a very strong current that flowed between two canyons and a crossroads where the black path was the one that led to Xibalba. From there, the deceased would find the council hall where the Lords of Xibalba sat, a garden of flowers and birds, the house of the supreme judge, a ballgame court, a sacred tree, a cliff, a fountain, and six houses of torment. Xibalba was located in the deepest part of the underworld; however, it did not encompass the entire subterranean world.

Recent ethnographic accounts show that the idea of an underworld is still alive in modern Maya

____

36 See Manzanilla (2021).

communities; however, their versions differ vastly from the original pre-Hispanic concept. A strong influence from Catholicism can be perceived in those modern conceptualizations of the underworld.

Other Realms of the Dead

It was believed that Tlaloc chose the individuals who died that way. The deceased were buried directly into the ground, as if they were seeds. The Maya had a place somewhat similar to the Tlalocan - it was called the Paradise of the Ceiba. It was a place of abundance and plenty and housed the souls of those who hanged themselves.

The Tarascans of Michoacan believed that the underworld was located underground; they called it Cumiechucuaro or "the place where one is with the moles." It was inhabited by gods that looked like people and animals and it was ruled by a mole named Uhcumo. Cumiechucuaro was divided into four sections corresponding to the four cardinal directions. The entrance was located to the east since that is where the sun rises. The Tarascans also had another land of the dead called Patzcuaro that could be entered through the lake of the same name.

This was a dark place and the destination of those who died by drowning. It was ruled by Chupi Tiripeme, the god of water.

In the Central Highlands, there was the belief in a place called Uarichao or "place of women," which housed the souls of women who died in childbirth. It was located to the west and ruled by Thiuime, The Black Squirrel.

Finally, the Mixtec of Oaxaca believed that the underworld was ruled by the god Pitao Pecelao. He was associated with death and illness, as well as wealth, luck, and the cultivation of the nopal cactus.[37] People would make offerings to him to reverse bad omens and alleviate illnesses.

The Beings of the Underworld

The Mesoamerican underworld was a place where many different kinds of beings lived. This section will discuss some of the main living elements associated with it, including mythical creatures, deities, animals, and even a plant.

---

[37] The nopal cactus, also known as prickly pear cactus, is an edible cactus widely available throughout Mexico. It was consumed regularly in pre-Hispanic times and its sap was used to make a kind of glue.

In Maya art, there are numerous representations of humans, animals or hybrid beings in the form of busts, heads, or full-body figures that are placed inside the open jaws of cosmic monsters. In many Mesoamerican civilizations, the role of cosmic monsters was to place actions and beings on the different planes of the universe, mainly the celestial and earthly realms, but for the Maya these depictions took on a slightly different role. In the Maya area, these representations typically appear over aquatic bands which place them in the wet underworld, such as in the pillars of Palenque's house D. Characters that appear in the center of a medallion formed by four lobes are in the realm of the dead or dry underworld, such as on the ballgame markers at Copan.[38]

In Maya representations of cosmic monsters, the jaws usually only contain one creature inside. The cosmological association of these beings is linked to either a movement or a situation. In both cases, they transmit a message which can be expressed in a dynamic or static way. In dynamic images, the jaws belong to an earthly or celestial monster and the

____

[38] For additional details on these examples, see Baudez (2005).

creature inside shows the action of being spit out or engulfed by the monster. For example, on stela N at Copan,[39] there are two kings shown inside the jaws of a crocodile and a toad respectively. The noble status of the first one is evident by his clothing and authority symbols. The second one, in contrast, wears no jewels and lacks a regal character. It is assumed that the first one is alive and coming out of the jaws, while the second one is dead and sinking into them. Static images don't show any kind of movement; their representations simply depict a character inside the jaws without any kind of action associated to it.

The idea of cosmic opposites can be found in many aspects of the pre-Hispanic system of beliefs. This was often represented in deities and signs that clashed to create a dynamic force in the universe, for example, the sun against the moon and stars; the forces of daylight, which included celestial and masculine energies, against the forces of the night, which included feminine and dark forces related to the underworld. However, there are two deities that combine both forces, representing harmony instead

---

[39] See Baudez (2005).

of a struggle between opposites. One of them is
Ometeotl "God 2," supreme deity of the Nahua
religion, and the other is Tlahuizcalpantecuhtli, the
planet Venus, which is the one of interest in relation
to the underworld.

Tlahuizcalpantecuhtli was represented as twin
brothers: Quetzalcoatl, the morning star, god of
light, of life and the celestial realm; and Xolotl, the
evening star, god of darkness, the underworld, and
death. Mesoamerican people were well aware that
these were two manifestations of the same star;
Venus' cycle was observed and traced with great
precision by Maya astronomers. Both aspects of
Tlahuizcalpantecuhtli were related to the sun since
Quetzalcoatl announced its rising and Xolotl was in
charge of transporting Tlachitonatiuh, the sun god,
across the underworld at night.

Xolotl is depicted as a dog, specifically the
xoloitzcuintli breed, native to Mexico. Just as Xolotl
accompanied the sun as is crossed the underworld,
so did a *xoloitzcuintli* dog accompany the dead on
their journey to Mictlan.

Xolotl had several attributes; he was the god of

twins and all things that were double. He had ties to the underworld and darkness, and he was the patron of witches and sorcerers. He could turn into the Mexican turkey or *huexolotl* whose meat was considered to be sacred, as was that of the *xoloitzcuintli*. He is also the patron of the seventeenth day sign *ollin*, which means movement. The sign is composed of two bands that are intertwined and symbolize harmony. In addition, Xolotl is also the god of the ballgame, which has been linked to the underworld and the battle of opposing sacred forces like, day-night, light-darkness, sun-moon, life-death, and masculine-feminine.

In an ancient myth, Xolotl was to be sacrificed along with other gods so that the Sun and Moon, which had just appeared in the sky, could begin their movement. The story says that Xolotl ran away scared trying to avoid being sacrificed. He hid first among maize plants and became the double maize called *xolotl*, then among maguey plants and turned into the double maguey called *mexolotl*, and then he went into the water and turned into the fish known as *axolotl*. Xolotl was eventually found and sacrificed. The accounts of this myth show him to be a dark and strange deity who participated in the creation of time and life in the universe; however, he is also credited with creating all the abnormal things in nature. Xolotl was charged with carrying the sun across the underworld at night, a very important mission in terms of the cosmic dynamic that puts into evidence that the darkness, the abnormal, and death are all essential parts of life.

In the Mesoamerican belief system, many animals held a sacred character; one of these was the jaguar. Though this animal was associated to the earthly realm, when it was represented as a supernatural being known as "the Jaguar in the Water Lily," it became the jaguar god of the underworld. In these representations, the jaguar wears a sacrificial scarf decorated with "eyes of death" and a corn plant with six leaves from which a head emerges in the form of a corn cob. This particular jaguar is associated with Maya sacrificial rituals, especially those of decapitation of war captives.

The jaguar was connected to the beginning and the end of times, as well as to the dark world in which it lives and rules. The sacred nature of the jaguar can be seen in many pre-Hispanic representations, such as in art, rituals, and myths. These representations can be found all across Mesoamerica, both in terms of space and time. In addition to its associations with political power and shamanic practices, the jaguar was also a creature related to night and the underworld, agriculture and fertility, and destruction and death.

The jaguar's characteristics place it in the realm of darkness, linked to the feminine side, the night, and the underworld. It holds a strong connection to the gods of the underworld and to many portals leading to this realm, such as caves, the inside of mountains, and deep dense forests and jungles. The feline exerts its power both on earth and below it; it is a powerful and dangerous animal that possessed special forms of otherworldly knowledge out of the reach of humans. When the jaguar is shown in combination with the celestial serpent, there is a clear link between the two realms.

Even though the underworld is considered to be the land of the dead, it is full of life and energy. The gods of death live there, along with many elements and nocturnal animals that represent the forces of that half of the cosmos, among which the jaguar stands out.

Scholars believe that the Maya image of the *huilz* monster, which means mountain, is a schematic representation of the jaguar's face with open jaws, signaling the entrance into the underworld. This connection is also supported by the fact that, in its natural environment, the jaguar often lives in caves which, in turn, are also considered portals to the underworld.

The jaguar's influence extends to the Maya ritual calendar or *tzolkin*, where days ruled by the feline were considered negative for any kind of social activity. The day *akbal*, which means night and darkness, is directly linked to the jaguar, as are the months *uo*, which symbolizes the dark sky and *pax*, which represents the nighttime sun. In particular, the associations of the nighttime sun with the jaguar are abundant among the Maya. Graphically, it is shown as a solar god with feline traits that can be the ears or spots and, on occasion, there is simply a glyph representing darkness. The connection between the jaguar and the nighttime is not exclusive to the Maya; in fact, it can be found all over Mesoamerica. It was believed that jaguars that crossed through the darkness swallowed any star in their path, leaving mankind without their light. It was the feline that embodied the destructive forces of the darkness, its unrefrained aggression that devoured the celestial bodies during eclipses as well. In Yucatec Maya, the word for eclipse is *chi'bil k'in,* which means "bite of the sun." The jaguar's association to the night can also be found throughout Mesoamerica in the comparison between the animal's spots and stars in the nighttime sky.

  Bats are typically associated to dark things, often linked to death and evil. In ancient Mesoamerica, these creatures were related to the underworld along with other creatures such as owls, scorpions, and spiders. Since at least 500 BCE, representations of bats can be found on sculptures, ceramic urns, codices, paintings, calendars, and even place names. The bat received different names in the many pre-Hispanic languages. In Nahuatl it was called *tzinacan,* in Maya *zotz,* in Zapotec *bigidiri beela* or *bigidiri zinia* (butterfly of flesh), in Mixtec *ticuchi lehle*, and in Huasteca *thut*.[40]

According to a Nahua myth, *tzinacan* was born from the semen and blood spilled by Quetzalcoatl during a self-sacrifice. The bat was then sent to bite off the genitals of the goddess Xochiquetzal and deliver them to the gods who then washed them. From that water, fragrant flowers grew. The genitals were then sent down to Mictlantecuhtli, Lord of the Underworld, who washed them again. From that water, the cempoalxochitl, flower of the dead, bloomed.

Some scholars interpret the bat as an animal that rips heads off since there are representations of the bat holding heads in its "hands." Maya codices show it holding a sacrificial knife in one hand and the victim in the other.

The lotus flower's connection to the aquatic realm is evident and, in pre-Hispanic times, it had countless symbols and meanings, forming part of transcendental aspects of the Mesoamerican worldview. The flower follows a daily

____

[40] Muñoz Espinosa (2006).

transformation similar to that of the sun, blooming during the day and disappearing at night, a situation that resonates with Mesoamerican mythology. In addition, the plant's rhizomes contain a powerful hallucinogenic substance that, when consumed, was believed to transport a person to the underworld; to the land of the ancestors.

The direct link between the lotus and the underworld can be found in artistic representations such as the murals of Bonampak.[41] In room 1, there is a scene that takes place in *Xibalba*, the Maya underworld, where six characters appear dressed as amphibians. They have been identified as lords of *Xibalba*. The characters represent ballgame players as well, who play a central role in creation myths because the game itself represented a confrontation between opposing cosmic forces. Most of the characters depicted in the mural have lotus flowers.

The lotus is associated to the wet underworld and the crocodile. On the mural, the flower appears on the central figure's crocodile headdress. There is an important visual relation between the flower and a

---

[41] See Uriarte (2005).

drum or *tunk'ul* that appears in the mural, and is also the glyph *tuun*. *Tuun* was the name of the year in which the mural was painted. A second drum is named *pax*, which corresponds to the name of the month in the Maya calendar and is related to the lotus flowers. As was mentioned above, the lotus was also associated to the jaguar in its form of "Jaguar in the Water Lily," which held a strong connection to the underworld.

Funerary Rites and Practices

Al throughout history, mankind has celebrated different kinds of rituals related to death as a social manifestation. The different rituals associated to death played a fundamental role in the social dynamic of ancient communities, reflecting their systems of values and beliefs.

The study of ancient Mesoamerica is divided into three main periods: Preclassic (1500 BCE – 300 CE), the Classic (300 – 950 CE), and the Postclassic (950 – 1521 CE). These periods correspond, in general terms, to developmental stages or times of important changes throughout the territory. In the case of the conception of death, the duality of life and death can be traced back to the middle Preclassic period.

The sources available that provide information on the Mesoamerican belief in the afterlife are scarce and they vary according to time period. For the Preclassic, most of the information comes from archaeological evidence recovered from funerary offerings found at sites such as: El Mirador, Izapa, Cuicuilco, and Tlatilco. The best evidence to support this is a clay mask that was found at the site of Tlatilco in the Central Highlands in which half of the face represents a living person and the other half is a skull. Burials corresponding to this period contain offerings and even the skeletal remains of dogs, highlighting the fact that many concepts related to the underworld were firmly established from the earliest times.

For the Classic period, the information is a bit more abundant including evidence from the burials of nobles, mural paintings, stelae, pottery, and inscriptions. In the Classic period, death was considered fundamental for the proper functioning of the cosmos. Death by ritual sacrifice became a widespread practice intimately linked to religion and political power. The idea of glorious death became quite relevant during this time and very vivid public displays of death, like the *tzompantli* or skull racks, can be found in several sites, including Tula and Chichen Itza.

The largest amount of data; however, comes from the Postclassic and Colonial periods due mainly to the presence of codices and ethnohistorical texts written by Spanish chroniclers. The interest of these Europeans in documenting funerary practices, ideologies, and beliefs concerning death and the underworld provide extremely valuable information.

Shaft tombs found in the western regions of Mesoamerica provide evidence of the importance of preserving family ties in the afterlife. The deceased were also typically buried with the tools they employed to carry out their jobs since they believed that they would continue to work in the underworld. Only during celebrations in honor of the dead could these souls return to earth, recovering their vital functions. That is why family members would prepare food for their dearly departed on these occasions. This tradition is still practiced in some indigenous communities, and similar beliefs can be seen during *Dia de Muertos* where relatives prepare the dead's favorite dishes so that they can feast at the altar set up in their honor. People say that the next day the food placed on the altars taste like nothing.

For the majority of the population, funerary rituals took place in the house. The remains of the deceased were often buried underneath the rooms of their households. The situation was quite different for those who belonged to the elite; their bodies were lavishly buried in sacred spaces located in the most important parts of their cities. One of the best examples is the tomb of Pakal in Palenque, Chiapas. The tomb contained a monolithic sarcophagus with an extremely detailed carving in which the deceased king is depicted with a maize plant emerging from his chest. Here, the connection between death and maize is apparent.

All throughout the Maya area there was (and still is) the belief that there was a system of underground roads or *sacbeob* that were used by the dead. During their journey on these roads, the soul had to take care of itself and feed itself, which is why tombs were equipped with food, talismans, and tools, and there was often a sacrificed dog also placed there to accompany his master and carry him over the river that separated Xibalba from the rest of the underworld. If the deceased was an important person, women and servants were also sacrificed and placed in the tomb. At the end of the journey, the person's spirit died for good and was incorporated into the realm of death, transformed into energy that would remain there for all eternity.

Spanish chronicler Motolinia dedicated an entire chapter of his memoirs to describing the funerals of the pre-Hispanic elite. He narrates that the deceased was watched over in his house for four days, after which a precious stone was introduced in their mouth and a strand of hair from the crown of their head was cut. The hair was placed in a box along with a strand that had been cut soon after their birth. The individual's face was then covered with a mask and the body was wrapped in luxurious cotton blankets. Attributes of the deity in whose temple they would be buried were placed on the body.

The mortuary bundle was taken to the foot of the main temple and burned with copal[42] and a torch. Numerous servants and slaves were sacrificed on the sacrificial stone and burned in another pyre so that their souls could accompany that of their lord. A dog was also sacrificed so that it could guide the deceased. Flowers and food were offered to the lord to make the journey more pleasant.

When the body had been consumed by the fire, priests collected the ashes and bits of bone left, along with the precious stone that had been placed in the lord's mouth and all was placed in the box that contained the strands of hair. The box was placed with a sculpture of the deceased and rich offerings were made during four days. After that time, the box was buried and a series of sacrifices and offerings were made to go along with the grieving ceremonies that ended after four years.

A burial was found in 1994 during the explorations of a building named House of the Eagles by the archaeologists working on the project.[43] This unique

---

[42] Copal is a resin burned as incense that was widely used in Mesoamerica and can be still found in Mexico nowadays.
[43] See Roman Berrelleza & Lopez Lujan (1999).

architectural complex had a privileged location within the great Aztec capital of Tenochtitlan. Just 15 meters north of the main pyramid, the Templo Mayor, rich decorations and a neo-Toltec style characterized the house. The archaeological findings shed interesting light on funerary practices and the underworld.

During the excavations, archaeologists uncovered several ceramic sculptures representing partly defleshed beings and characters dressed with eagle costumes, mural paintings in the style of codices, benches with multicolored reliefs, and lavish offerings.

The burial described in the following paragraphs was found in the third constructive phase of the House of the Eagles, dating back to the last two decades of the 15th century, corresponding to the rule of the Aztec emperors Tizoc or Ahuizotl. The interment ceremony took place at the foot of a staircase that led up to the eastern wing of the building where three cylindrical pits were dug. In each pit a ceramic vessel was placed that contained the partial remains of a single individual, as well as rich offerings.

This triple funerary deposit contained the cremated remains of several beings: one human, one dog, one jaguar, one royal eagle, and one sparrow hawk. In addition, the offerings contained ceramic objects, obsidian, flint, basalt, green stone (jade), turquoise, gold, copper, bronze, pyrite, bone, shell, copal, cotton, and palm. In total, the collection of artifacts came to 101 complete pieces and 350 fragments.

The three large ceramic vessels used as funerary urns were among the most impressive pieces in the collection. Each piece corresponded to a different time period; the oldest among them corresponded to the Late Classic period and contained representations of the well-known butterfly man typical of Teotihuacan iconography. The second one was an effigy pot in the form of an old man's head that dated back to the Early Postclassic period. Finally, the third vessel was a large polychrome flagon from the Late Postclassic that had an elaborate decoration of beads, flowers, hearts, and geometrical designs.

The human remains were found both inside and

outside the urns. Despite the damage and deterioration the bones had gone through due to the effects of the cremation fire and the natural processes of decomposition, archaeologists were able to determine that all the fragments belonged to one individual, an adult male. The bone fragments and ashes of the aforementioned individual were accompanied by animals and objects that were commonly found in burials, not only in Tenochtitlan, but also in nearby sites like Tlatelolco and Tenayuca. Some of the most impressive items contained in the offering were the remains of a dog which, as has been previously discussed, was an animal that was often buried with the deceased to guide them to the underworld, a circular bead made out of green stone, several obsidian beads shaped in the form of duck heads, an obsidian ring, several flint and obsidian arrowheads, pieces of copal resin, and cords made out of cotton and palm fibers.

  The deceased's body was also accompanied by objects that were used exclusively by the nobility. Among them were the charred remains of at least three items of clothing that were made out of the finest cotton and decorated with embroidery. There were also numerous pendants, gold plate decorations in circle and half-moon shapes that may have belonged to one of the garments, bronze and copper bells, turquoise mosaics, and copper pins. The last two were likely part of a crown or nasal decoration. Crowns and ornaments were often placed on the mortuary bundles of lords and warriors who died heroically. Finally, the most unique artifacts found during the archaeological excavations were two fangs that had been intentionally trimmed. They were identified by a biologist as belonging to an adult jaguar and scholars believe that they were given to the deceased as amulets or insignias of power and status.

Detailed analysis of the burial remains allowed archaeologists to learn several things about the dead individual. The fact that the body was cremated and the presence of dog bones and a bead made of green stone – which would have been placed in the individual's mouth – are clear indicators that this was a case of *tlalmiquiztli* or natural death. The incineration rite had the purpose of liberating the deceased's *teyolia* so that it could journey to

Mictlan. It is also evident that this person possessed a very high status in the Aztec society due to the wealth expressed in the offerings and the location of the burial in a sacred space. While the identity of the individual remains unknown, the evidence points to the possibility that he was a lord or *tecuhtli* or a high ranking military officer.

The Mesoamerican concept of the afterlife includes a complex system of beliefs and worldview that differs considerably from the European one. While western religion promotes the idea of an afterlife conditioned by the way an individual acted during their life, pre-Hispanic cultures had the notion of a "land of the dead" or underworld where the souls of most individuals journeyed upon death. The Mesoamerican underworld has been compared to the Christian concept of hell; however, the two are completely different.

For ancient Mesoamericans, the underworld was one of three realms of existence. They believed the world to have three planes: the celestial realm, the earthly realm, and the underworld. The pre-Hispanic vision of the underworld varied slightly from culture to culture. For societies living in central Mesoamerica, the underworld was called Mictlan and was ruled by Mictlantecuhtli, the Lord of Death. In the Maya area, the land of the dead was known as Xibalba and it was ruled by a series of deities. Despite their differences, these two conceptions of the underworld shared several characteristics. They were both said to have nine levels or layers that the deceased had to cross in order to reach the deepest level – Mictlan or Xibalba – and each of these levels presented the dead with a trial that had to be overcome.

Other similarities include the belief that certain natural elements were doors or portals to the underworld. Caves and water features, like lakes and cenotes, were the most commonly used geographical landmarks associated with entrances to the land of the dead. Caves had ritual uses that were also linked to funerary rites, sacred burials and ritual offerings. Additionally, caves were conceived as the mouth of the great earth monster which was also connected to the complex beliefs related to death.

The underworld was also compared to the female

womb since there was a strong connection between death and life. Pre-Hispanic cosmology conceived the universe as a cyclical process in which opposing forces were necessary for it to function. Day and night, male and female, sun and moon, and life and death were all connected as integral parts of the universe. With that in mind, death was not a permanent condition in the Mesoamerican worldview, but a transition or continuation of life; a process of renewal that transformed into fertility and new life.

There were many animals, mythological creatures, deities, and plants associated to the underworld as well. Some of the most relevant were Xolotl, the nocturnal aspect of the planet Venus, the cosmic monster (or earth monster), the jaguar, the bat, and the lotus flower. Each of these played an important role in the overall functioning of the underworld and the universe as a whole.

The evidence available on the Mesoamerican conceptions of the underworld comes from archaeological data, codices, and ethnohistorical accounts. Though largely incomplete, these sources provide at least a partial understanding of the pre-Hispanic view on death. Hopefully, future research and findings will allow Mesoamerican historians and archaeologists to construct a more complete picture of the pre-Hispanic concepts of the afterlife and underworld.

Online Resources

Other books about ancient history by Charles River Editors

Further Reading

Baudez, C. F. "En las fauces del monstruo." Arqueología Mexicana, núm. 71, 2005, pp. 58-67.

Bernal Romero, G. "Cuevas y pinturas rupestres mayas. Ti' Ik' Way-nal, 'en el lugar del abismo negro.'" Arqueología Mexicana, núm. 93, 2008, pp. 35-40.

Campaña, L. E. & Boucher, S. "Nuevas imágenes de Becán, Campeche." Arqueología Mexicana, núm. 56, 2002, pp. 64-69.

Cartwright, M. "Mictlantecuhtli." World History Encyclopedia, 2013. Retrieved from:

https://www.worldhistory.org/Mictlantecuhtli/

Cartwright, M. "Xibalba." World History Encyclopedia, 2014. Retrieved from: https://www.worldhistory.org/Xibalba/

Chavez Balderas, X. Afterlife: Mesoamerican Concepts. Cengage. 2005. Retrieved from: https://www.encyclopedia.com/environment/encyclopedias-almanacs-transcripts-and-maps/afterlife-mesoamerican-concepts

De la Garza, M. "La muerte y sus deidades en el pensamiento maya." Arqueología Mexicana, núm. 40, 1999, pp. 40-45.

De La Garza, M. "El carácter sagrado del xoloitzcuintli entre los nahuas y los mayas." Arqueología Mexicana, núm. 125, 2014, pp. 58-63.

Dupey García, E. "De vírgulas, serpientes y flores. Iconografía del olor en los códices del Centro de México." Arqueología Mexicana, núm. 135, pp. 50-55. 2015

Earley, C. C. "The Mesoamerican Ballgame." In Heilbrunn Timeline of Art History. New York: The

Metropolitan Museum of Art, 2017. Retrieved from: http://www.metmuseum.org/toah/hd/mball/hd_mball.htm

Escartin Arroyo, R. "Xibalba y Mictlan." Una comparación sobre el inframundo en Mesoamérica. Diplomado en Estudios Mexicanos, Universidad Nacional Autónoma de México, 2014.

Heyden, D. "Las cuevas de Teotihuacán." Arqueología Mexicana, núm. 34, 1998, pp. 18-27.

Johansson, P. "La muerte en Mesoamérica." Arqueología Mexicana, núm. 60, 2003, pp. 40-53.

López Austin, A. "Misterios de la vida y de la muerte." Arqueología Mexicana, núm. 40, 1999, pp. 4-9.

Luna Lopez, M. "El camino al Mictlan: ¿ruta al tormento o al origen?" Vita Brevis, Revista electrónica de estudios de la muerte, num. 11, 2017, pp. 159-172. Retrieved from: https://revistas.inah.gob.mx › index.php › vitabrevis › article › download › 11698 › 12466

Manzanilla, L. "El concepto de inframundo en

Teotihuacán." El cuerpo humano y su tratamiento mortuorio, Centro de estudios mexicanos y centroamericanos, 2021, pp. 127-143. Retrieved from: https://books.openedition.org/cemca/2517

Matos Moctezuma, E. "Los mexicas y la muerte." Arqueología Mexicana, edición especial núm. 52, 2013, pp. 18-20.

Matos Moctezuma, E. "El largo viaje al Mictlan y los números 4 y 9." Arqueología Mexicana, edición especial núm. 52, 2013, pp. 28-30.

Mikulska, K. "Los cielos, los rumbos y los números. Aportes sobre la visión nahua del universo." In Cielos e inframundos. Una revisión de las cosmologías mesoamericanas, 2015, pp. 109-174. Universidad Nacional Autónoma de México. Retrieved from: http://www.historicas.unam.mx/publicaciones/publicadigital/libros/cielos/inframundos.html

Muñoz Espinosa, M. T. "El culto al dios Murciélago en Mesoamérica," Arqueología Mexicana, núm. 80, 2006, pp. 17 - 23.

Moyes, H. "Constructing the Underworld: The

Built Environment in Ancient Mesoamerican Caves." Association for Mexican Cave Studies, no. 23, 2012, pp. 95-110.

Moyes, H. "Rites in the Underworld: Caves as Sacred Space in Mesoamerica." Mexicolore, July 24, 2013. Retrieved from: https://www.mexicolore.co.uk/aztecs/home/caves-as-sacred-spaces-in-mesoamerica

Pereira, G. "Arqueología de un lugar de pasaje hacia el inframundo." Las Ciencias Sociales y la Muerte, num. 58, 2010, pp. 19-28. Retrieved from: https://journals.openedition.org/trace/1524.

Román Berrelleza, J. A. & López Luján, L. "El funeral de un dignatario mexica." Arqueología Mexicana, núm. 40, 1999, pp. 36-39.

Salas Cuesta, M. E. & Talavera González, J. A. "Una visión de la vida y de la muerte en el México prehispánico." Arqueología Mexicana, núm. 102, 2010, pp. 18-23.

Uriarte, M. T. "¿Son las ninfeas un símbolo solar en Mesoamérica?" Arqueología Mexicana, núm. 71, 2005, pp. 68-71.

Valverde Valdés, M. C. "El jaguar entre los mayas. Entidad oscura y ambivalente." Arqueología Mexicana, núm. 72, 2005, pp. 47-51.

Vela, E. "La muerte." Arqueología Mexicana, edición especial núm. 75, 2017, pp. 59-61.

Free Books by Charles River Editors

We have brand new titles available for free most days of the week. To see which of our titles are currently free, click on this link.

Discounted Books by Charles River Editors

We have titles at a discount price of just 99 cents everyday. To see which of our titles are currently 99 cents, click on this link.